T5-CVF-598

ECONOMICS
AND
SOCIETY

THEOLOGY OF WORK ▸ PROJECT

ECONOMICS
AND
SOCIETY

THE BIBLE AND YOUR WORK
Study Series

HENDRICKSON
PUBLISHERS

Theology of Work
The Bible and Your Work Study Series: Economics and Society

© 2016 by Hendrickson Publishers Marketing, LLC
P.O. Box 3473
Peabody, Massachusetts 01961-3473

ISBN 978-1-61970-806-8

Adapted from the *Theology of Work Bible Commentary*, copyright © 2014 by the Theology of Work Project, Inc. All rights reserved.

All Scripture quotations, unless otherwise indicated, are taken from the Holy Bible, New Revised Standard Version (NRSV), copyright © 1989, National Council of the Churches of Christ in the United States of America. Used by permission. All rights reserved.

Scripture quotations marked (NASB) are taken from the New American Standard Bible®, Copyright © 1960, 1962, 1963, 1968, 1971, 1972, 1973, 1975, 1977, 1995 by The Lockman Foundation. Used by permission. (www .lockman.org)

William Messenger, Executive Editor, Theology of Work Project
Sean McDonough, Biblical Editor, Theology of Work Project
Patricia Anders, Editorial Director, Hendrickson Publishers

Contributors:

Valerie O'Connell and Leah Archibald, "Economics and Society" Bible Study
Clint Le Bruyns, Theology of Work Project original materials

The Theology of Work Project is an independent, international organization dedicated to researching, writing, and distributing materials with a biblical perspective on work. The Project's primary mission is to produce resources covering every book of the Bible plus major topics in today's workplaces. Wherever possible, the Project collaborates with other faith-and-work organizations, churches, universities and seminaries to help equip people for meaningful, productive work of every kind.

Printed in the United States of America

First Printing—July 2016

Contents

The Theology of Work

Work is not only a human calling, but also a divine one. "In the beginning God created the heavens and the earth." God worked to create us and created us to work. "The LORD God took the man and put him in the garden of Eden to till it and keep it" (Gen. 2:15). God also created work to be good, even if it's hard to see in a fallen world. To this day, God calls us to work to support ourselves and to serve others (Eph. 4:28).

Work can accomplish many of God's purposes for our lives—the basic necessities of food and shelter, as well as a sense of fulfillment and joy. Our work can create ways to help people thrive; it can discover the depths of God's creation; and it can bring us into wonderful relationships with co-workers and those who benefit from our work (customers, clients, patients, and so forth).

Yet many people face drudgery, boredom, or exploitation at work. We have bad bosses, hostile relationships, and unfriendly work environments. Our work seems useless, unappreciated, faulty, frustrating. We don't get paid enough. We get stuck in dead-end jobs or laid off or fired. We fail. Our skills become obsolete. It's a struggle just to make ends meet. But how can this be if God created work to be good—and what can we do about it? God's answers for these questions must be somewhere in the Bible, but where?

The Theology of Work Project's mission has been to study what the Bible says about work and to develop resources to apply the

Christian faith to our work. It turns out that every book of the Bible gives practical, relevant guidance that can help us do our jobs better, improve our relationships at work, support ourselves, serve others more effectively, and find meaning and value in our work. The Bible shows us how to live all of life—including work—in Christ. Only in Jesus can we and our work be transformed to become the blessing it was always meant to be.

To put it another way, if we are not following Christ during the 100,000 hours of our lives that we spend at work, are we really following Christ? Our lives are more than just one day a week at church. The fact is that God cares about our life *every day of the week*. But how do we become equipped to follow Jesus at work? In the same ways we become equipped for every aspect of life in Christ—listening to sermons, modeling our lives on others' examples, praying for God's guidance, and most of all by studying the Bible and putting it into practice.

This Theology of Work series contains a variety of books to help you apply the Scriptures and Christian faith to your work. This Bible study is one volume in the series The Bible and Your Work. It is intended for those who want to explore what the Bible says about work and how to apply it to their work in positive, practical ways. Although it can be used for individual study, Bible study is especially effective with a group of people committed to practicing what they read in Scripture. In this way, we gain from one another's perspectives and are encouraged to actually *do* what we read in Scripture. Because of the direct focus on work, The Bible and Your Work studies are especially suited for Bible studies *at* work or *with* other people in similar occupations. The following lessons are designed for thirty-minute lunch breaks (or perhaps breakfast before work) during a five-day work week.

Christians today recognize God's calling to us in and through our work—for ourselves and for those whom we serve. May God use this book to help you follow Christ in every sphere of life and work.

Will Messenger, Executive Editor
Theology of Work Project

Introduction

Economics is at the heart of every society. Economic systems span from entrepreneurial capitalism to communal socialism in an array as diverse as humanity itself. Whatever the form, when economies prosper or falter, lives are directly affected for good or for ill. Meanwhile, the topic of economics encompasses a variety of concerns from the lowly household budget to questions of international trade. From the micro- to the macro-level, economics relates to a wide breadth of disciplines and issues that impact our world today.

In our participation in economic systems, as in all spheres of life, Christians are called to the peace of God, the joy of the Lord, and fullness of life. Referring to the people who would hear his voice, Jesus told his disciples, "I came that they may have life, and have it abundantly" (John 10:10). In this abundant life, we as Christians are called to flourish, not just survive. We are invited to enjoy a fullness of life in which there is dignity and purpose. Regardless of our financial state or social station, Christians can experience personal significance through our identity as God's children, adopted by means of Jesus' sacrifice. And yet, the Good News does not allow us to ignore economic structures in our current world that demean others, or economic practices that exploit the environment without long-term vision. Nor does our inheritance through Jesus allow us to abdicate our responsibility to work. Rather, the Christian calling requires that we engage with economic questions, to ensure that all creation benefit from principled economic exchange. We are God's children *in* the world.

Called to live the abundant life in a fallen world, we nonetheless face the reality of economic hardship and the many issues it presents. Jesus observed, "For you always have the poor with you, but you will not always have me" (Matt. 26:11), stating a reality that millions face every day. But through our work, we can make a difference. As workplace Christians, we are committed to God's life-giving mission amid life-denying situations. We seek opportunities for active and constructive engagement with our world.

This Bible study brings a biblical perspective to the study of economics, with the overarching mission of increasing fullness of life for all people. Looking to fundamental principles established in the Old and New Testaments, this study focuses on ways Christians can engage with economic questions to make wise decisions and take helpful actions.

Many lessons in this study will encourage you to think about an economic problem, without providing you with specific answers, positions, politics, or solutions. You will learn six approaches to engaging with economics: prophetic, narrative, technical/ethical, policy, participatory, and invitational. Through these approaches you will learn how to wrestle with tough questions. You will be called to answer for yourself these questions: How does Christian faith guide us in the realm of economics? And how can we best advance a more abundant life for all?

Chapter 1

Faith, Work, and Economics

Lesson #1: Your Faith Is a Public Faith

Our convictions about God matter. Our public role as Christians in society is important when we consider the relationship between Christian faith and economic life. Matthew 5:14–16 captures this well:

> You are the light of the world. A city built on a hill cannot be hid. No one after lighting a lamp puts it under the bushel basket, but on the lampstand, and it gives light to all in the house. In the same way, let your light shine before others, so that they may see your good works and give glory to your Father in heaven.

Thus by definition our faith is a public matter. Yes, it is grounded in our personal response to Jesus, but it does not remain private. The theology and ethics that stem from our faith are also public. What we believe about God or humanity or the future is not an abstract belief system, but is the basis for our engagement with all areas of life. What we believe has direct implications for everyday life and work.

The church as a whole also serves a public function, not just as a locally worshiping congregation, but as a civic participant at community, national, and global levels. Therefore the mission of Christians is a public mission. In light of the Great Commission (Matt. 28:16–20), our agenda is not congregational or denominational growth, but the realization of God's kingdom here on earth in all our relationships with people and with the broader creation.

The impact of our actions is also public. What we believe and how
we act as Christians affects other people in all spheres of life.

 Food for Thought

When Jesus said "I came that they may have life, and have it abundantly" (John 10:10) he was talking about the fullness of life, not
material possessions. What would your abundant life look like if
you were able to define it? What role does material comfort play
in this picture for you?

— Dynamic relationships w family, friends

— Abiding trust + obedience in rel w God

— Meaningful pastoral work

—

Your faith is a public faith because people are always weighing
your words and your actions and because the results of your work
affect the world around you. It is often easier to love your neighbor
in the privacy of your own home than in the reality of a shared
driveway. How well does your personal commitment to Jesus
match your public actions?

_____

_____

_____

_____

How deeply do you invest in relationships with the people you work with every day? If the answer were measured by how much you pray for them, then how would it change your care for them? Take a moment to pray for the specific needs and concerns of one of your co-workers.

_____

_____

_____

_____

_____

_____

_____

_____

_____

Prayer

Lord,

Thank you for offering me not only life but abundant life. I ask that your grace be alive and vital in my personal and public life today. Let my actions bring glory to my Father in heaven and hope to my neighbors and friends.

Amen.

Lesson #2: Work-Grounded Economics

The world of economics is grounded in the world of work. The words *economy* and *economics* can conjure up images of abstract and complicated ideas, which tend to discourage us from giving much thought to the topic. But as workplace Christians, we can grow our faith and our effectiveness by a biblical understanding of economics, society, and our work.

Derived from the Greek words *oikos* (house) and *nomos* (law, rule, custom), economics is concerned with the management of resources within the household—our own and that of God's creation. It begins with work. Whatever we do to produce or procure the things we want and need is work. Any kind of productive work is part of the economy. Homebuilders, homemakers, nurses, and managers all work, whether for pay or not, and therefore have direct experience with the economy.

As Christians committed to living out our faith in all aspects of life, we have the right and even the responsibility to reflect on our participation in the economy. We should consider several levels of economics in this reflection.

- The macro-dimension of economics is concerned with global and systemic issues. Macroeconomics can help us understand the productive capability of businesses and nations, the causes of global financial crises, or the complex impacts of economic globalization in different parts of the world, for example.

- Throwing the spotlight on mid-level institutional and organizational issues turns attention to business ethics, practices, and organizational policies in our places of work.

- The micro-dimension of economics is relevant to our concerns about personal and local income, debt, prices, and systems of exchange.

As workplace Christians committed to God's life-giving mission amid life-denying situations, our view is informed by Jesus' mission, as described in John 10:10. "The thief comes only to steal and kill and destroy. I came that they may have life, and have it abundantly." The work of the Triune God throughout Scripture and beyond has been to make fullness of life a greater reality for all God's creation. We share in this mission through our work and the roles we play in economics and society.

 Food for Thought

Is *economics* a word that makes you feel disconnected in a way that the word *work* does not? Does one seem practical while the other seems abstract?

_____

_____

_____

_____

_____

_____

_____

It is natural to hold a view or position on matters that are local or personal. But as Christians who are called to put others first, we need to look past our individual borders and comfort levels that distance us from the concerns of others. What you do on a personal level at work has impact on how well your organization performs. How often or seriously do you consider the role of your work and your decisions in the greater welfare of others?

Prayer

    God,

    Please help me to see the role of my work in your economy, that I may be faithful in all my dealings for the good of all.

                                               Amen.

Lesson #3: Your Work Has Worth

Our work has economic worth whenever it is productive work. Whether paid or on a volunteer or nurturing basis, productive work is directed at the social good, aimed at what we need and want for a more abundant life. Although economics has a technical dimension to it, the world of economy is fundamentally a social activity grounded in the world of work in which we all have experience. It is useful to think of our work as contributing to greater fullness of life—our own and that of others.

The economic sphere is included in the Christian claim that God is present in all aspects of our lives. The fact that all aspects of life are subject to God's judgment and to God's grace is a call to discern his will for all of our activities. The transforming presence of the Holy Spirit is with us in all our activities, and there is no situation in which we cannot call upon and expect God's help. The economic activities in which we engage are a vital part of our lives as God's people.

We must also acknowledge that sin has compromised us and introduced ambiguity, even contradictions, to our beliefs and actions. We must recognize the bad as well as the good in our public witness, especially as far as economic matters are concerned.

For instance, while we affirm the goodness of God's creation, as a society we have both cared for and harmed the environment. We affirm the sovereignty of God, but recognize that we have demonstrated both loyalty to God and idolatry to wealth. As Christians, we ask the question of how to manage our Christian faith and economic life from a position of confession, acknowledging ambiguity in our public role in history. Sin remains all too real.

At work, we can add to the fullness of life when we pay attention to others' needs, including the need to be respected. When we set aside our privileges to joyfully serve others and work for their good with no expectation of return, we add value and we follow the example of Jesus.

 Food for Thought

Recognizing that your work has real worth, what would your workplace look like if you tried to bring others joy through the way you treat them? In what ways do you treat your co-workers and clients as people of value and dignity? What can you do today to bring joy to someone in your workplace?

_____

_____

_____

_____

_____

_____

_____

Do you believe that the economic activities in which we engage are a vital part of our lives as God's people? If you do, in what ways do you demonstrate that belief? If you don't, then take a moment to consider how this compartmentalization might be putting distance between you and God. Is this an area where you feel better having God on the outside?

_____

_____

_____

_____

_____

_____

_____

_____

Prayer

Father,

You have called us to fullness of life in our work life as well as in our worship life. Please help me to receive my work as a gift from your hands and as an opportunity to improve the lives of my co-workers and clients today.

Amen.

Chapter 2

Bible-Based Economics

Lesson #1: Yes, Economics Is for You Too

Workplace Christians are sometimes hesitant to engage with economic issues, partly because we may not see how we can have a meaningful and constructive role to fulfill in the economic arena. We may be intimidated by economics. If we see the topic as deeply complex, then we can suffer from a "complexity paralysis," in which we lack confidence in addressing economic questions.

But we all have personal economic experiences that provide insight into larger economic systems and their potentials and problems. For instance, we know that at some point borrowing cannot be endless or without consequences. We know that it feels much better to be actively engaged in employment than to have to accept charity. We understand buying and budgeting, plenty and want, security and fear.

As such, we have an experience base from which to approach economic issues. As followers of Jesus, we also have the authority to criticize or praise economic systems that affect our lives and the lives of others near and far. When those systems cause others injustice or pain, we have the responsibility to exert that authority.

Economics must be seen in its proper place. Economic exchange—buying, selling, making, consuming, saving, and borrowing—is simply one realm of the things people do. While economics explains many aspects of human life, to overvalue its importance puts us in danger of putting love of money before love of God and people. To undervalue economics, on the other hand, is to walk away from our rightful authority and voice in an important area of our societies.

 *Food for Thought*

How is reflecting on work, economic life, and society important and relevant in terms of living faithfully?

_____

_____

_____

_____

_____

Do you agree or disagree that you have the baseline knowledge and right to make judgments about economic matters that impact society? Does your household budget and buying experience give you any meaningful insight into how your local or national governments are running their affairs? Does it matter to you? Why or why not?

_____

_____

_____

_____

_____

_____

Picture this choice: You need to buy a winter coat for each person in your family this year, and your finances are tighter than usual. Your local store is running a huge sale on just the type of coats you need, saving you hundreds of dollars. But you wonder whether the coats are inexpensive because they were made by workers who were paid low wages in a country wracked with poverty. You think, "Well, the labor was already used. I can't undo what's been done. And I can't afford to get new coats at full price." Do you buy the coats?

_____

_____

_____

_____

_____

_____

_____

Prayer

Dear God,

I am beginning to suspect that there is a whole area of my life in which I could better serve you. Please help me to see the ways that I can make a difference in my workplace and in my understanding of economic issues that impact society. You are the God of the marketplace as well as the church, and I want to serve you and your people. Thank you that I live in a time and place to pursue these questions.

Amen.

Lesson #2: In the Beginning, There Was Work and Economics

The Bible is far from being a treatise on economics. But it is equally far from being silent on the matter. Beginning in Genesis 2:15, God makes it clear that work is intended to be part of creation: "Then the Lord God took the man and put him into the garden of Eden to cultivate it and keep it" (NASB). Cultivation is one of the most basic economic activities. Like the rest of God's creation, the relationship between man and work was designed to be good, even very good. It was not until after the Fall that work became toil: "And to the man he said, 'Because you have listened to the voice of your wife, and have eaten of the tree about which I commanded you, "You shall not eat of it," cursed is the ground because of you; in toil you shall eat of it all the days of your life'" (Gen. 3:17).

Later, when God set about building a nation, a people for himself, he gave Moses laws to be followed—many of which had to do with work, economics, and society at large. The earliest commandments include the requirement to rest: "Remember the sabbath day, to keep it holy. Six days you shall labor and do all your work, but the seventh day is a sabbath of the Lord your God; in it you shall not do any work, you or your son or your daughter, your male or your female servant or your cattle or your sojourner who stays with you" (Exod. 20:8–10 NASB).

Accustomed as we are to modern labor laws governing working conditions, we may not see how revolutionary the Sabbath was in the context of its time. God, who had designed that humanity should work, mandated rest as a requirement for the society he was building when he brought Israel out of Egypt. Not only were his people to rest on the Sabbath, but so also were servants, working animals, and strangers in the land. Even the land itself was to rest. God ordained a sabbath year, one in every seven (Lev. 25:1–7), in which each field was to lie fallow.

It is clear that God intended his people both to work and to rest in a sacred rhythm. This balance was a defining aspect of the society he was building. How serious God was about observing the Sabbath becomes clear in Numbers 15:35, when a man who had ignored the injunction was brought to judgment. "Then the LORD said to Moses, 'The man shall surely be put to death; all the congregation shall stone him with stones outside the camp'" (NASB). It was the responsibility of all the people to participate in both observing the laws and administering the penalty for breaches.

 Food for Thought

What role does the concept of "Sabbath" play in your life? Do you take the requirement to rest as seriously as you take the need to work? Does the idea of dedicating a day to rest have any vitality today, or is it a quaint artifact from simpler times?

_____

_____

_____

_____

_____

_____

_____

_____

What are some of the ways that a society's view of work impacts or shapes its values? In some cultures hard work is admired; in others it is looked at as lower class. How does the society you live in shape your view of your work? Do you value some professions more than others?

_____

_____

_____

_____

_____

_____

_____

_____

Prayer

Dear God,

Please forgive me for the times I have placed my work above my worship of you. Help me to bring balance into all of my relationships in my workplace, my home, and communities.

Amen.

Lesson #3: The Economy at Rest

Just as the land had a sabbath rest every seven years, the entire economy was to enjoy a jubilee year every fifty years. Every fiftieth year, all leased or mortgaged lands were to be returned to their original owners, and all slaves and bonded laborers were to be freed: "You shall thus consecrate the fiftieth year and proclaim a release through the land to all its inhabitants. It shall be a jubilee for you, and each of you shall return to his own property, and each of you shall return to his family" (Lev. 25:10 NASB).

The purpose of the jubilee year was to maintain a social and economic balance within Israel's twelve tribes. After Israel conquered Canaan, the land was assigned to Israel's clans and families (see Num. 26; Josh. 15–22). This land was never to be sold in perpetuity, for it belonged to the Lord, not the people (Lev. 25:23–24).

The effect of the jubilee was to prevent any family from becoming permanently landless through sale, mortgage, or permanent lease of its assigned land. In essence, any sale of land was really a term lease that could last no longer than the next year of jubilee (Lev. 25:15). The existence of the jubilee year provided a means for the destitute to raise money (by leasing their land) without depriving the family's future generations of the means of production.

The jubilee year has many angles of interest:

- *Theologically*, the jubilee affirms that the Lord is not only the God who owns Israel's land; he is sovereign over all time and nature. His act of redeeming his people from Egypt committed him to provide for them on every level because they were his own. Therefore, Israel's observance of the Sabbath day and year and the year of jubilee was a function of obedience and trust.

- *Socially,* the smallest unit of Israel's kinship structure was a household that would have included three to four generations. The jubilee provided a socioeconomic solution to keep the family whole, even in the face of economic calamity.

- *Economically,* two principles are revealed that we can apply today. First, family units must have the opportunity and resources to provide for themselves. Second, God desires just distribution of the earth's resources. According to God's plan, the land of Canaan was assigned equitably among the people. The jubilee was not about redistribution but restoration.

 Food for Thought

The jubilee year required that the Israelites trust God to provide for their immediate needs and for the future of their families. It also called on the rich to treat debtors compassionately, trusting that God would yield an adequate return. What part does trust play in your economic view?

_____

_____

_____

_____

_____

_____

_____

_____

Then as now, the effects of family debt included a frightening list of social ills. The jubilee sought to check these negative social consequences by limiting their duration. What impact does multigenerational poverty have today? Who should care, and what should they do about it?

_____

_____

_____

_____

_____

_____

_____

_____

Prayer

> *Father,*
>
> *There is nothing I have that is not from you. Help me to hold my possessions with a jubilee spirit of worship and obedience. Thank you for everything I have.*
>
> *Amen.*

Chapter 3

Rights and Responsibilities at Work

Lesson #1: Gleaning for the Rich and the Poor

> "When you reap the harvest of your land, you shall not reap to the very edges of your field, or gather the gleanings of your harvest. You shall not strip your vineyard bare, or gather the fallen grapes of your vineyard; you shall leave them for the poor and the alien: I am the LORD your God." (Lev. 19:9–10)

> "When you reap your harvest in your field and forget a sheaf in the field, you shall not go back to get it; it shall be left for the alien, the orphan, and the widow, so that the LORD your God may bless you in all your undertakings. When you beat your olive trees, do not strip what is left; it shall be for the alien, the orphan, and the widow. When you gather the grapes of your vineyard, do not glean what is left; it shall be for the alien, the orphan, and the widow. Remember that you were a slave in the land of Egypt; therefore I am commanding you to do this." (Deut. 24:19–22)

Gleaning is the process of picking up heads of grain or pieces of fruit that remain in a field after harvesters have passed through. According to God's covenant with Israel, farmers were not allowed to glean their own fields, but were to allow poor people to glean them as a way of supporting themselves. God limited the rights of Israelite farmers and landowners in three key ways:

1. They were to leave the margins of their grain fields un-harvested. The width of this margin appears to have been the owner's decision.

2. They were not to pick up whatever produce fell to the ground. This restriction applied when a harvester grasped a bundle of stalks and cut them with the sickle, as well as when grapes fell from a cluster just cut from the vine.

3. They were to harvest their vineyards once, presumably taking only the ripe grapes and leaving the later ripening ones for the poor and the immigrants living among them.

The result of these laws was to extend the right of both the poor and the rich to earn a living—the poor through work and the rich through the economics of farming—to the benefit of their society.

 Food for Thought

Gleaning required the poor to work for their support, effectively performing their own mini-harvest. How does this arrangement differ from charity?

_____

_____

_____

_____

_____

The gleaning laws called on those who owned the means of production to provide opportunities for work and sustenance to the poor. Are there comparable factors at work today?

_____

_____

_____

_____

_____

_____

_____

_____

Why did God tie these gleaning laws to a reminder that he is "the LORD your God" and that "you were a slave in the land of Egypt"? Is there something God has done for you that spurs you to action whenever it comes to mind?

_____

_____

_____

_____

_____

_____

_____

Prayer

Lord,

Thank you for the balance in your creation. I praise you that you are mindful of both the rich and the poor. Teach me to exercise my rights with generosity and my responsibilities with grace.

Amen.

Lesson #2: Generosity Is Not Optional

The gleaning laws gave poor people access to the means of production necessary to support themselves and their families. In general, every family (except among the priestly tribe of Levites, who were supported by tithes and offerings) was to have a perpetual allotment of land that could never be taken away (Num. 27:5–11; 36:5–1; Deut. 19:14; 27:17; Lev. 25). Thus everyone in Israel would have the means to grow food.

But foreigners, widows, and orphans typically did not receive an inheritance of land, so they were vulnerable to poverty and abuse. The gleaning law gave them the opportunity to provide for themselves. Laws benefiting the poor were common in the ancient Near East, but only the regulations of Israel extended this treatment to the resident foreigner. This provision was yet another way that God's people were to be distinct from the surrounding nations.

The gleaning system created an opportunity for the poor to work (by gleaning the fields) rather than having to beg, steal, starve, or sell themselves into slavery. Gleaning was a way to participate in the dignity of work, even for those who were unable to participate in the labor market due to lack of resources, socioeconomic dislocation, discrimination, disability, or other factors. God wants everyone's needs to be met, but he also wants to offer everyone the dignity of working to meet their needs and the needs of others.

These passages in Deuteronomy 24 about gleaning suggest three guidelines for partnering with the poor in economic activity:

1. Providing work for the poor is a prerequisite to God blessing the work of people's hands (v. 19);

2. Creating an economy where everyone benefits from meaningful work is to be driven by the memory of Israel's experience under cruel and abusive slave masters in Egypt (v. 22a); and

3. Partnering with the poor in reciprocal economic relation-
    ships is a matter of obedience to the will of God (v. 22b).

 Food for Thought

In what ways do gleaning laws apply to us? In today's developed
economies, each one of us is a person of means, even if we are not
rich. Do middle class people have the means and the responsibility
to provide opportunities for poor people? How about poor people
themselves?

_____

_____

_____

_____

_____

_____

In a world in which every nation and every society has under- and
unemployed people in need of opportunities for work, how can
Christians use the concepts of gleaning to bring God's blessing of
fruitfulness to other workers and would-be workers?

_____

_____

_____

_____

_____

_____

Picture this situation: You have been assigned to lead a project that will bring you lots of recognition and opportunities for advancement if completed successfully. You are also allowed to choose the members of your team. Among the potential team members are some new employees of your organization, whose capabilities and experience you don't know. Do you choose any of them to join the team, or only co-workers whom you know personally to have a proven track record?

_____

_____

_____

_____

_____

_____

_____

_____

Prayer

   Jesus,

   You gave up every right in order to give me life. Please grow your generosity in my heart so that I may share every blessing with my co-workers, family, and neighbors.

                                                    Amen.

Lesson #3: Work Is Not Charity

From the outside, following the gleaning laws may look like an expression of compassion or justice, but according to Leviticus, allowing others to glean on our property is the fruit of holiness, done because God said, "I am the LORD your God" (Lev. 19:10). This command highlights the distinction between charity and gleaning. In charity, people voluntarily give to others who are in need, and the people on the receiving end are dependent upon the givers to keep on giving. Charity is not what Leviticus is about.

Gleaning places an obligation on landowners to provide poor and marginalized people access to the means of production (in Leviticus, the land) and on the poor to work it themselves. Unlike charity, it does not depend on the generosity of landowners. In this sense, it was much more like a tax than a charitable contribution. Also unlike charity, it was not given to the poor as a transfer payment. Through gleaning, the poor earned their living the same way as the landowners did, by working the fields with their own labors. It was simply a command that those without their own land be given access the means of provision created by God.

Work is not charity. In the gleaning system, the landowner's obligation to offer access met with the worker's responsibility to work. This balance made the difference between charity and work, which in turn respected workers' dignity and developed their capacity, skills, and habits of work.

No individual business owner can provide opportunities for every unemployed or underemployed worker, any more than any one farmer in ancient Israel could provide gleanings for the entire district. But are today's owners called to be the point people in providing opportunities for work? Or has this responsibility passed to governments alone? Perhaps we as Christians are called to both support business owners as job-creators in their communities and remind them of their accountability in this role.

 *Food for Thought*

Modern society may not be well-suited to gleaning in the literal, agricultural sense, but are there aspects that can be incorporated into ways societies care for poor and vulnerable people today? In particular, how can we provide opportunities for people to gain access to the means of productive work, rather than being smothered by dependency or exploitation?

_____

_____

_____

_____

_____

_____

_____

_____

Consider that access to education, capital, product and job markets, transportation systems, and nondiscriminatory laws and regulations may be what poor people need to be productive. Christians disagree with each other about questions such as individual versus social responsibilities, private versus public means, and income distribution. In what ways could you apply the concepts of gleaning to today's social, political, and theological debates about poverty and the private and public responses to it?

_____

_____

_____

———————————————————————

———————————————————————

———————————————————————

———————————————————————

———————————————————————

Prayer

Father,

Today I ask that you bless the job-creators in our society with an increasing awareness of the love and the power of Jesus in their lives and in their businesses. Thank you for your provisions.

Amen.

Chapter 4
The Right to Fairness

Lesson #1: Judging Others Fairly

> "You shall not render an unjust judgment; you shall not be partial to the poor or defer to the great: with justice you shall judge your neighbor. You shall not go around as a slanderer among your people, and you shall not profit by the blood of your neighbor: I am the LORD." (Lev. 19:15–16)

This short section from Leviticus upholds the familiar biblical value of justice, and then broadens it considerably. The first verse begins with an application for judges, but ends with an application for everyone. Do not judge court cases with partiality, and don't judge your neighbor unfairly. The wording of the Hebrew highlights the temptation to judge the external appearance of a person or issue. Woodenly rendered, Leviticus 19:15 says, "Do not do injustice in judgment. Do not lift up the face of the poor one and do not honor the face of the great one. With rightness you shall judge your neighbor." Judges must look past their preconceptions (the "face" they perceive) in order to understand the issue impartially.

The same is true of our social relationships at work, school, and civic life. In every context, social biases of all kinds create injustice. The latter part of Leviticus 19:16 reminds us that social bias is no light matter. Literally, the Hebrew says, "Do not stand by the blood of your neighbor." In the language of the courtroom in the previous verse, biased testimony ("slander") endangers the life ("blood") of the accused. In that case, not only would it be wrong to speak biased words, but it would also be wrong even to stand by without offering to testify on behalf of one falsely accused.

Leaders in workplaces must often act in the role of an arbiter. Workers may witness an injustice in the workplace and legitimately question whether or not it is appropriate to get involved. Leviticus claims that proactively standing in favor of the mistreated is an essential element of belonging to God's holy people. On a larger level, Leviticus brings its theological vision of holiness to bear on the whole community. Partnering with the marginalized through just economic relationships benefits the health of the entire community.

 Food for Thought

Imagine the difference Christians could make if we simply waited to make judgments until we knew people and situations thoroughly. What would change if we took the time to know those annoying people on our team instead of complaining about them?

_____

_____

_____

_____

_____

_____

_____

_____

Do you spend time with people outside of your comfort zone at school, work, or civic life? Do you ever seek out newspapers, television programs, or other media that offer different perspectives from yours? Would digging below the surface give you greater wisdom to do your work well and justly?

_____

_____

_____

_____

_____

_____

_____

Picture this situation: Layoff rumors are everywhere. It is not time to rock the boat. A co-worker who has caused you plenty of trouble in the past has been accused of harassment. You know that in this one instance he is wrongly accused. What do you do?

_____

_____

_____

_____

_____

_____

_____

Prayer

Father,

Help me to look past my biases to an authentic impulse toward your justice and love. Strengthen me to stand beside those in need and protect those unfairly endangered.

Amen.

Lesson #2: Fairness in Customer Relationships

Differences of class and wealth can create opportunities for injustice. Justice requires treating poor people as fairly as rich. "You shall not withhold the wages of poor and needy laborers, whether other Israelites or aliens who reside in your land in one of your towns" (Deut. 24:14). Justice also requires treating customers fairly. "You shall not have in your bag two kinds of weights, large and small" (Deut. 25:13). The weights in question are used for measuring grain or other commodities in a sale. For the seller, it would be advantageous to weigh the grain against a weight that was lighter than advertised. The buyer would profit from using a falsely heavy weight. But Deuteronomy demands that a person always use the same weight, whether buying or selling. Protection against fraud is not limited to sales made to customers, but it extends to all kinds of dealings with all the people around us. Deuteronomy 27 is clear on multiple points:

- Cursed be anyone who moves a neighbor's boundary marker (v. 17).

- Cursed be anyone who misleads a blind person on the road (v. 18).

- Cursed be anyone who deprives the alien, the orphan, and the widow of justice (v. 19).

- Cursed be anyone who takes a bribe to shed innocent blood (v. 25).

Economic thought and actions have value and impact our society. Our ethical and moral positions should invade every aspect of our businesses, including marketing plans, sales strategies and tactics, as well as product development and hiring practices. Every kind of workplace—home, business, government, academia, medicine, agriculture, and all the rest—has a distinctive role to play in the fabric of society. Similarly, all spheres of society are improved when individuals are trustworthy in their economic decisions.

In modern terms, injustice might include a company that ignores the moral implications of knowingly selling a defective product, customers who abuse store policies by returning used merchandise, or workers who conduct personal business or ignore their work during paid time. Not only are these practices unjust, but they also violate the commitment to worship God alone, "for you to be a people holy to the LORD your God" (Deut. 26:19).

 Food for Thought

Are people treated equally in your workplace? Or are some more equal than others? Are double standards employed between those who are favored and those who are not? What kinds of metrics are used to measure employees, managers, customers, suppliers, and others? Are they fair?

_____

_____

_____

_____

_____

_____

_____

If you had free rein to determine the policies and principles at your work, what would you change to more closely align with your Christian values? Is there any area within your control where you could bring more fullness of life? How would that change work for others?

_____

_____

_____

_____

_____

_____

_____

Prayer

Jesus,

It is so easy to separate my deeply held beliefs and loyalties to your word from my day to day actions on the job. I ask that your Holy Spirit increasingly guide me to make the two perfectly aligned so that I may be an agent of your justice everywhere I have a voice.

Amen.

Lesson #3: Fairness in Employee Relationships

A troubling topic in Deuteronomy is slavery. Israelites became slaves to one another not through kidnapping or at birth, but because of debt or poverty. In those cases, slavery was preferable to starvation. People sold themselves into slavery to pay off a debt, but neither the debt nor the slavery was endless. "If a member of your community, whether a Hebrew man or a Hebrew woman, is sold to you and works for you six years, in the seventh year you shall set that person free" (Deut. 15:12). Upon release, former slaves were to receive a share of the wealth their work had created. "When you send a male slave out from you a free person, you shall not send him out empty-handed. Provide liberally out of your flock, your threshing floor, and your wine press, thus giving to him some of the bounty with which the LORD your God has blessed you" (Deut. 15:13–14).

Today, although desperate workers are not generally sold into involuntary labor, they can be desperate enough to take whatever jobs they are able to find. Because their desperation makes them vulnerable to exploitation and abuse, modern employers frequently abuse them in ways similar to the ways ancient masters abused slaves. Vulnerable workers today may face demands to work extra hours without pay, to turn over tips to managers, to work in dangerous or toxic conditions, to pay petty bribes in order to get shifts, to suffer sexual harassment or degrading treatment, to receive inferior benefits, or to endure illegal discrimination and other forms of mistreatment. The fact that Deuteronomy contains protections for slaves makes it logical to extend those protections to all workers now.

Deuteronomy requires that masters abide by contract terms and labor regulations including the fixed release date, the provision of food and shelter, and the responsibility for working conditions. Work hours must be reasonably limited, including a weekly day off (Deut. 5:14). Most significantly, masters are to regard slaves as equals, remembering that all God's people are rescued slaves. "Remember that you were a slave in the land of Egypt, and the LORD your God redeemed you; for this reason I lay this command upon you today" (Deut. 15:15).

 Food for Thought

There are places where people are still sold (usually by parents) into debt bondage—a form of work that is slavery in all but name. Others may be lured into sex trafficking, from which escape is difficult or impossible. Christians in some places are taking the lead in rooting out such practices, but much more could be done. Imagine the difference it would make if more churches and Christians made this cause a high priority for mission and social action. What can you do to help the cause of desperate workers in abusive employment?

_____

_____

_____

_____

_____

_____

_____

How does your view of God's position on work, economics, and society inform your view of issues such as the minimum wage, health care, and immigration? What other issues come to mind? Do you feel God calls for balance or radical action?

_____

_____

_____

_____

_____

_____

_____

_____

Prayer

God,

I need your wisdom to know how I can help abused and exploited people—whether near or far, young or old. I need your love to give me the passion to put your justice into action.

Amen.

Chapter 5

Economic Relationships

Lesson #1: Civic Planning for Levitical Towns

Once in the Promised Land, each tribe was assigned a specific territory to hold in permanent trust. Unlike the rest of the tribes, the Levites were to live in towns scattered throughout the land. There they could teach the people the law and apply it in local courts. Numbers 35:2–5 details the amount of pasture land each Levitical town should have:

> You shall measure, outside the town, for the east side two thousand cubits, for the south side two thousand cubits, for the west side two thousand cubits, and for the north side two thousand cubits, with the town in the middle. (v. 5)

The plan accommodates growth. Mathematically, as the town grows, so also does the area of its pasture land, but at a lower rate than the area of the inhabited town center. That means the population is growing faster than agricultural area. For this growth to continue, agricultural productivity per square meter must increase. Each herder must supply food to more people, freeing more of the population for industrial and service jobs. This outcome is exactly what is required for economic and cultural development. To be sure, the town planning doesn't cause productivity to increase, but it creates a socioeconomic structure adapted for rising productivity. It is a remarkably sophisticated example of civic policy creating conditions for sustainable economic growth.

This passage in Numbers 35 illustrates again the detailed attention God pays to enabling the human work that sustains people and creates economic well-being. The fact that God instructed Moses on civic planning based on semi-geometrical growth of pastureland suggests that he values all aspects of human life. All the professions, crafts, arts, academics, and other disciplines that sustain and prosper communities and nations are godly pursuits for God's people of today.

 Food for Thought

Do you think that some professions or actions are viewed as more God-honoring than others? Is there any reason to believe that excellence in city planning, economics, child care, or customer service bring less glory to God than heartfelt worship, prayer, or Bible study?

_____

_____

_____

_____

_____

_____

In our churches, do we actively encourage and celebrate fellow Christians' excellence in all fields of endeavor? Would you do anything differently if you viewed excellence at your work as a way of serving our Lord?

_____

_____

_____

_____

_____

_____

_____

_____

It is easier to effect change from inside an organization or institution than from the outside. Protesters can stand outside of a company's headquarters shouting slogans and waving signs all day long, but the doors remain barred and the policies unchanged. By contrast, one well-placed executive can make a big difference. What arenas can you influence at your work?

_____

_____

_____

_____

_____

_____

_____

_____

Prayer

Father,

Thank you that you care about all aspects of our lives. I want to increasingly view my work as a service to you, and excellence as a form of worship, that I may bring joy to others and glory to you.

Amen.

Lesson #2: The Rich Play a Godly Role in Society

Deuteronomy requires owners of productive assets to employ those resources for the benefit of the community. Not surprisingly, the requirements are sensible, practical, and fair to both the rich and those reliant upon them. For example, landowners were to allow neighbors to use their land to help meet their immediate needs.

> If you go into your neighbor's vineyard, you may eat your fill
> of grapes, as many as you wish, but you shall not put any in a
> container. If you go into your neighbor's standing grain, you may
> pluck the ears with your hand, but you shall not put a sickle to
> your neighbor's standing grain. (Deut. 23:24–25)

This law was the provision that allowed Jesus' disciples to pluck grain from local fields as they went on their way (Matt. 12:1).

God requires us to be open with our resources to those in need, while also exercising good stewardship of the resources he entrusts to us. On the one hand, everything we have belongs to God, and his command is that we use what is his for the good of the community (Deut. 15:7). On the other hand, Deuteronomy does not treat a person's field as common property. Outsiders could not simply cart off as much as they pleased. The requirement for contribution to the public good is set within a system of private ownership as the primary means of production.

God, however, directs people in control of assets to be fair:

> "Do not withhold good from those to whom it is due, when it is in your power to do it. Do not say to your neighbor, 'Go, and come back, and tomorrow I will give it,' when you have it with you." (Prov. 3:27 NASB)

> "You shall not oppress a hired servant who is poor and needy, whether he is one of your countrymen or one of your aliens who is in your land in your towns. You shall give him his wages on his day before the sun sets, for he is poor and sets his heart on it; so that he will not cry against you to the LORD and it become sin in you." (Deut. 24:14–15 NASB)

Private ownership carries the responsibility for public good.

 Food for Thought

We're so often tempted to treat what we have been given as our own. What particular resources do you find the hardest to consider yourself a trustee of and not an owner? Why?

_____

_____

_____

_____

_____

_____

_____

_____

Wealth can prevent people from recognizing the humanity of the rich. Some people overvalue the wealthy, trying to curry favor with them and prizing their opinions, while others paint them as oppressors who are less noble than the downtrodden. Where do you stand on this continuum? Is there clear biblical guidance for your viewpoint?

_____

_____

_____

_____

_____

_____

_____

Regardless of your absolute financial circumstances, if you have access to this book, you are wealthy in comparison to the circumstances of many people. What responsibilities does God put on you as a rich person?

_____

_____

_____

_____

_____

_____

Prayer

Jesus,

You put aside all of your power and riches to serve us. Show me ways that I can better serve your people and purposes with my resources—and grow my desire to do so.

Amen.

Lesson #3: Work, Worship, and the Environment

The prophet Haggai connects the economic and social well-being of the people with the state of the environment. By means of a play on words that is more obvious in Hebrew than in the English translation, Haggai links the desolation of the temple, "in ruins" (Hebrew *hareb*; 1:9), with the desolation of the land and its harvests, "drought" (Hebrew *horeb*), and the consequent ruination of the general wellness of "human beings and animals, and on all their labors" (1:11).

The linchpin of this link is the health of the temple, which becomes a symbol for the religious faithfulness or unfaithfulness of the people. So there is a three-way link between worship, socioeconomic health, and the environment. When there is disease in the physical environment on which we depend, there is disease in human society. When the environment is not protected, those who live or work on the land suffer economically. Finally, people have trouble experiencing full spiritual health when they become estranged from God's creation.

There is also a link between the way a community worships God and cares for the land, and the economic and political condition of those who occupy the land. The prophets all call us to relearn respect for both the earth we occupy and its creator. There are consequences for failing in this. For Haggai, the drought of the land and the ruin of the temple are inseparable. When people stray from God's ways, they degrade the land. When they return to true and wholehearted worship, peace and blessing from the land are restored. "Since the day that the foundation of the LORD's temple was laid, consider: Is there any seed left in the barn? Do the vine, the fig tree, the pomegranate, and the olive tree still yield nothing? From this day on I will bless you" (Hag. 2:18–19).

Given the importance of work and work practices to the well-being of the environment, if Christians were to do their work according to God's plan, we could have a profoundly beneficial impact on the planet and all those who inhabit it. It is the environmental responsibility of the faithful to learn tangible ways to do so.

 Food for Thought

Haggai delivers a long oracle on purity (2:10–19) in which he suggests a link between purity and the health of the land. Purity entails a fundamental respect for the integrity of the whole created order, the health of its ecospheres, the viability and well-being of its species, and the renewability of its productivity. How can we as Christians promote responsible environmental practices?

_____

_____

_____

_____

_____

_____

_____

One possible application of this concept is that a pure environment means an environment treated in sustainable ways by those to whom God has given responsibility for its well-being. Environmental issues can be seen as issues of personal morality, communal ethics, global interest, or business policy. How do your beliefs inform your positions on proper treatment of the environment? Consider the idea that peace with God includes care for the earth that he has made. How can you make any difference in this matter?

_____

_____

_____

_____

_____

_____

_____

_____

Prayer

God,

Thank you for your beautiful creation. I confess that I am not always grateful for it or careful with it. Please help me to gain a rightful understanding of how my work can care for your earth.

Amen.

Chapter 6

Bible-Based Economic Engagement

Lesson #1: Economics in a Fallen World

The examples we've covered in this study demonstrate that God is interested in the sphere of life called economics. From the gleaning laws to the jubilee year through the planning of Levitical towns, God has demonstrated that he cares greatly about justice, opportunity, and the rights and responsibilities of rich and poor people alike. Everyone should be able to earn a living with dignity, to contribute to the flourishing of society, and to enjoy fullness of life.

Even as God established that the owners of economic capital are to provide opportunity for workers to earn a living, Paul reaffirms that those given the opportunity must work: "If anyone is not willing to work, then he is not to eat, either" (2 Thess. 3:10 NASB). This balance of mutual responsibilities should work seamlessly. Unfortunately, free will and sin add complexity to real world systems. We cannot expect the Bible to present us with simple solutions on how to engage with modern economic problems. Rather, we can expect Scripture to give us frameworks to make decisions for ourselves in today's complex world. In the next lessons, we will introduce six biblical frameworks that guide us in engaging with economic problems. These are: prophetic, narrative, ethical, policy, participatory, and invitational. Through active engagement with theology in the context of our economic decisions, we can contribute life-giving witness to the everyday world.

Food for Thought

Do you notice a tendency to compartmentalize economic matters away from your Christian walk and worship? What challenges do you face in integrating all aspects of your faith?

_____

_____

_____

_____

_____

_____

Does Paul's admonition to the Thessalonians "If anyone is not willing to work, then he is not to eat, either" sound harsh or fair to you? How do our current systems empower or enfeeble people's willingness to work?

_____

_____

_____

_____

_____

_____

_____

How are God's interest and your responsibilities in work, economics, and society related?

_____

_____

_____

_____

_____

_____

_____

_____

Prayer

God,

Thank you for all you have given me. Help me to understand not only my responsibilities but also my abilities to make a difference as I engage with economic issues.

Amen.

Lesson #2: Prophetic Engagement

In the Bible, God calls prophets to engage the structures of society, especially kings and others in power, to reform the purposes and practices they pursue. Typically, this approach comes through a mixture of criticism of the current state of affairs and revisioning of the future.

Prophetic engagement involves the familiar language of criticism, confrontation, indictment, and challenge. It involves reading the Bible and reading the social context, and amid economic ill-being saying, "The picture of our present-day context is not how God intended it to be. It is not a picture of the good life for which Jesus came. Our status quo and God's vision of our economic life do not match." So it is when in James 5:1–4 we read condemnation of unjust behavior and fraudulent practices:

> Come now, you rich people, weep and wail for the miseries that are coming to you. Your riches have rotted, and your clothes are moth-eaten. Your gold and silver have rusted, and their rust will be evidence against you, and it will eat your flesh like fire. You have laid up treasure for the last days. Listen! The wages of the laborers who mowed your fields, which you kept back by fraud, cry out, and the cries of the harvesters have reached the ears of the Lord of hosts.

In Isaiah 65:17–19 we encounter a helpful example of the other side of the prophetic way, where we move from rebuke to revisioning. The passage reflects a dreaming about what economic life could be:

> For I am about to create new heavens and a new earth; the former things shall not be remembered or come to mind. But be glad and rejoice forever in what I am creating; for I am about to create Jerusalem as a joy, and its people as a delight. I will rejoice in Jerusalem, and delight in my people; no more shall the sound of weeping be heard in it, or the cry of distress.

Prophetic engagement seeks to energize by way of a new vision. It has a sense of paradise in mind, envisioning a new reality that matches God's vision of what economic life ought to be like. For many workplace Christians, biblical expressions of hope sustain their faith in a God who promises quality of life in the face of overwhelming life-denying circumstances for countless people throughout the world, especially in vulnerable workplace contexts in Latin America, Africa, and Asia.

 *Food for Thought*

The dual roles of rebuke and revisioning are both carried out on the platform of God's commands and promises. How can you effectively engage a nonbelieving audience of people who place no value on God or his purposes?

_____

_____

_____

_____

_____

_____

_____

What situation at your workplace or in your community lends itself to prophetic engagement? How would you frame the challenge, rebuke, and revision?

_____

_____

_____

_____

_____

_____

_____

Prayer

Dear Lord,

I ask for discernment to see injustice and the boldness to address it in confident faith.

Amen.

Lesson #3: Narrative Engagement

In narrative engagement we tell stories to move, inform, inspire, and embolden. Stories have power. They say something about the vision, values, and practices of a community. They illustrate and embody what we hold dear. Stories and storytelling abound in the Scriptures across narratives of the Israelites' journey, the boldness of the prophets, Jesus in his parables, and Paul in his Epistles.

We engage narratively all the time in the course of our Christian activities. Telling our stories and listening to the stories of others help us connect our faith and economic life. As we listen to other people's stories, we learn about such things as overcoming the odds against a background of poverty, or the harsh realities of someone struggling with unemployment, or the pleasure of creating opportunities to work. Very often these narrative encounters speak more convincingly to us and through us than more direct means of confrontation and communication.

Consider the approach the prophet Nathan took when rebuking King David for his treacherous combination of adultery and murder. Rather than walking into the throne room with judgment, he told his king the following story:

> "The rich man had a great many flocks and herds. But the poor man had nothing except one little ewe lamb which he bought and nourished; and it grew up together with him and his children. It

would eat of his bread and drink of his cup and lie in his bosom, and was like a daughter to him. Now a traveler came to the rich man, and he was unwilling to take from his own flock or his own herd, to prepare for the wayfarer who had come to him; rather he took the poor man's ewe lamb and prepared it for the man who had come to him." (2 Sam. 12:2–4 NASB)

Infuriated by the obvious treachery and injustice of these actions, David hurls his judgment: "As the LORD lives, surely the man who has done this deserves to die. He must make restitution for the lamb fourfold, because he did this thing and had no compassion" (2 Sam. 12:5–6 NASB). To this verdict, Nathan replies, "You are the man!" Stories can get past defenses in a way that direct judgment cannot.

 Food for Thought

Christians can learn useful insights from stories of social movements. Such movements usually arise when conditions reach a crisis point and ordinary people put aside risk to make changes happen. Can you think of a story that helped form a value or passion in your life?

_____

_____

_____

_____

_____

_____

_____

_____

Social movements represent crucial opportunities for ordinary people to criticize, identify with, support, reason with, understand, conceptualize, strategize, mobilize, organize, and carry out appropriate actions for social change. How can the church act as a transforming space for workplace Christians in their narrative engagement with economic life?

Picture a situation in your workplace that could really use reform or improvement. Try phrasing your response to it in two ways: as a demand or criticism, and as a story with a suggested ending.

Prayer

Jesus,

Thank you for speaking in parables that your disciples could clearly understand. I ask for your grace in telling stories that have meaning.

Amen.

Chapter 7

More Varieties of Engagement

Lesson #1: Technical or Ethical Engagement

In ethical or technical engagement we take a more scholarly approach. We get involved in the tasks of analyzing and clarifying. Here we raise conceptual and philosophical questions, as well as those of meaning and logic.

We engage in a technical sense with issues of Christian faith and economics when we read the Bible with a studying eye, looking at topics such as the nature and meaning of poverty, slavery and freedom, work and economic development, and financial investment. Although students, academics, and reflective practitioners commonly employ this approach, it has use for workplace Christians as well.

Three questions can assist us within the ethical discourse about economic life. As we read the Bible and explore what content we can offer as workplace Christians, we ask:

- What does a good economic society look like (vision)?

- How do economically moral people behave (virtues)?

- What are economically good decisions (actions)?

When we grapple with questions of vision, we are concerned with defining what elements, policies, systems, provisions, and institutions go into making a good economic society. When we grapple with questions of virtues, we are concerned with identifying the characteristics and attributes of morally good values and character. And when we pose questions about practices, we look for actions, decisions, and outcomes that are good for economic life. Across all areas of inquiry, people of faith are looking for practical ways to live out their faith commitments. Christians turn to biblical values to inform modern responses.

 Food for Thought

Technical engagement with the Bible reveals difficult truths, like the fact that God intends all people to work and not just receive charity (2 Thess. 3:10). An honest assessment of Scripture negates the practice of using the Bible to merely legitimize current economic practices. How do you respond to these issues when you read the Bible? What informs your vision for a good economic society?

_____

_____

_____

_____

_____

_____

Theologian Douglas Hicks focuses on nine specific economic practices for workplace Christians to consider: surviving, valuing, discerning desires, providing, laboring, recreating, expanding the community, doing justice, and sharing. Take a moment to note which of these actions have relevance to your workplace and community.

_____

_____

_____

_____

_____

_____

_____

What aspects of your workplace are most challenging to your
ability to wholeheartedly act in accordance with your values and
beliefs? What virtues affect your economic decisions?

_____

_____

_____

_____

_____

_____

_____

Prayer

Jesus,

*You lived a perfect and sinless life. May your Holy Spirit
guide my thinking and my steps to follow you with all my
heart, soul, mind, and strength.*

Amen.

Lesson #2: Policy Engagement

Policy engagement is a way of influencing public decisions about economic activity on a local, national, or international scale. Christians in positions of power should be particularly intentional about the way they influence economic policies. But policy engagement does not always require high position. Nehemiah held the trusted but lowly position of "cupbearer to the king" (Neh. 1:11), and he became a leader with great influence and access. He used that influence to commission and equip the work of rebuilding the wall around Jerusalem.

Policy engagement can be a challenging area. As churches and as Christians, we must be cautious of how we manage power relationships with government and business. We want to avoid potential situations in which the Christian vision is co-opted to fulfill the agendas of others. When this happens, we dilute or even lose our prophetic edge and function.

For instance, too often workplace Christians in less-developed countries find that the church as an institution acts like an elite enterprise that alienates them as working poor people. It is not uncommon to encounter theology of work initiatives that focus on the calling of leaders without any meaningful engagement with ordinary workers. In those situations, it is not surprising that workplace believers experience suspicion where there should be fellowship.

Another challenging aspect to policy engagement is that Christians are often not equipped to deal with the complex issues of policy formulation. For this reason, many withdraw from concerns about public policy and political matters. However, in order for Christians to make a meaningful difference in areas of economics, it is important that we view our leadership roles as roles that extend beyond congregational life into the public realm. This requires training in the economic disciplines, rather than retreating into church-dominated spheres. When we have a sectarian mentality, we deliver a fragmented ministry, a divided witness, and an impotent gospel for the world of work. The area of policy engagement offers an opportunity for workplace ministries and churches to back their biblical advice with intentional action and meaningful results.

 Food for Thought

Some workplace Christians serve on boards, think tanks, global committees, and similar decision-making structures within public life. Others participate in consultations and conferences that inform policy decisions. Some are members of government or conduct research that informs public opinion. Can you impact policy in any way?

_____

_____

_____

_____

_____

_____

_____

_____

All Christians can engage in economic policy-making, locally if not internationally. Interacting with public policy presents an active gospel to the world of work. How can you extend your influence beyond congregational life into the public realm? How can you prepare yourself to participate meaningfully in these realms?

_____

_____

_____

_____

_____

_____

_____

_____

Prayer

God,

I ask that you open my eyes to ways in which I can bring your love to policies in my community.

Amen.

Lesson #3: Participatory and Invitational Engagement

Participatory engagement calls on our ability to cultivate concern for others that leads to a shared sphere of behavior. The Bible commands us to love our neighbor. In economic terms this means working with other people across divisions of class or opportunity, to exchange labor and property through mutually-beneficial economic transactions.

Ephesians 4 describes this participatory relationship among Christians as an expression of unity, belonging, and partnership.

> The gifts he gave were that some would be apostles, some prophets, some evangelists, some pastors and teachers, to equip the saints for the work of ministry, for building up the body of Christ, until all of us come to the unity of the faith and of the knowledge of the Son of God, to maturity, to the measure of the full stature of Christ. (Eph. 4:11–13)

There are many different occupations represented in the body of Christ, but all must work together in economic activity that is beneficial to all members.

Invitational engagement rests on the capacity to bring divided or alienated people together based on a shared commitment to equality and self-determination. Our economic arena is comprised of many divisions and disparities—the rich and the poor, the educated and the uneducated, the "somebodies" and the "nobodies," the old and the young—the list is long. Amid such polarization, different groups often talk past each other. As Christians, we reflect an invitational engagement in economic life whenever we bear convening power—the ability to bring the most unlikely candidates together to work together in economic exchanges that connect people across such divisions. Employment, investment, and access to markets are all ways that Christians can invite others into empowering economic relationships. By definition, invitational engagement is also reciprocal. A fair exchange of labor and property benefits all parties.

 *Food for Thought*

In 2 Corinthians 5:18–19, Paul writes,

> Now all these things are from God, who reconciled us to Himself
> through Christ and gave us the ministry of reconciliation, namely,
> that God was in Christ reconciling the world to Himself, not
> counting their trespasses against them, and He has committed to
> us the word of reconciliation. (NASB)

In what ways are the participatory and invitational engagements
acts of reconciliation? Think of groups at work or in your community who could benefit from reconciliation. Do you have a role
to play?

_____

_____

_____

_____

_____

_____

_____

We see that differences can either polarize groups or strengthen
and build up community, as in Ephesians 4:11–13. What makes
the difference between polarization and strengthening?

_____

_____

_____

_____

_____

_____

_____

_____

When we think of divisive topics, religion and politics immediately come to mind. On what lines are the topics of economics and economic policy likely to break down into divisions?

_____

_____

_____

_____

_____

_____

_____

_____

Prayer

Jesus,

Make me an ambassador of reconciliation. Give me the ability to listen with respect and understanding, and the grace to speak your words of peace and forgiveness.

Amen.

Chapter 8

Working for the Good of Others

Lesson #1: We Are a City Set on a Hill

As workplace Christians, we are both economic actors and citizens of God's kingdom. In Matthew 5:14–16 Jesus says:

> "You are the light of the world. A city set on a hill cannot be hidden; nor does anyone light a lamp and put it under a basket, but on the lampstand, and it gives light to all who are in the house. Let your light shine before men in such a way that they may see your good works, and glorify your Father who is in heaven." (NASB)

We are called to be visible wherever we are—whether at work or in our communities. Being visible requires investment in the well-being of our neighbors. This includes economic investment in others, creating value beyond our close circle of fellow Christians. Similarly, Christian businesses and households should demonstrate biblical values by producing more than we consume. A debt-ridden world needs to see those who possess the fruits of the Spirit, including self-control, demonstrate responsible economic practices grounded in faith.

God's people can bless any workplace, institution, or organization we are a part of. This has always been true. When the Babylonians sacked Jerusalem and carried Israel into captivity, God had his prophet Jeremiah charge the people with seeking good for the cities of their exile:

"Build houses and live in them; and plant gardens and eat their produce. Take wives and become the fathers of sons and daughters, and take wives for your sons and give your daughters to husbands, that they may bear sons and daughters; and multiply there and do not decrease. Seek the welfare of the city where I have sent you into exile, and pray to the LORD on its behalf; for in its welfare you will have welfare." (Jer. 29:5–7 NASB)

Like the captive Israelites, we bring light to the world today when we produce, develop businesses, work, provide work for others, pray, and seek God's fullness of life for everyone we encounter.

 Food for Thought

The psalmist recalled Israel crying out from the shores of Babylon, "How can we sing the LORD's song in a foreign land?" (Ps. 137:4 NASB). Why did God command his people to seek the welfare of the cities in their exile? Are you called to seek the welfare of your workplace or town?

_____

_____

_____

_____

_____

_____

_____

_____

Think about being part of God's city, wherever you are. Regardless of the view out your window, you are not alone. Your fellow citizens are in every walk of life in every place around the world. Take a moment to pray for their well-being. Maybe someone is praying for you. Write down your thoughts here.

_____

_____

_____

_____

_____

_____

_____

_____

Prayer

Dear Father,

Let your light shine through me in such a way that others may see your good works, and glorify you in heaven and on earth.

Amen.

Lesson #2: Create Opportunity for People in Need

We cannot ignore the practical needs of others in our communities. James asks:

> If a brother or sister is without clothing and in need of daily food, and one of you says to them, "Go in peace, be warmed and be filled," and yet you do not give them what is necessary for their body, what use is that? (James 2: 15–16 NASB)

He does not have to wait for an answer to this rhetorical question. Wishing someone in need well is useless. We are not to be observers of the word, but "doers of the word, and not merely hearers who deceive themselves" (James 1:22).

We bear a responsibility for the immediate needs of those around us. But how does that inform a globalized Christian response to poverty? Many Christian charitable programs have had a backfiring effect on the most impoverished people throughout the world. Programs that merely transfer goods or funds from one group to another cultivate a culture of dependency that perpetuates the cycle of poverty from one generation to the next. A deeper commitment to the poor for whom Christ died demands that we use whatever resources we have not only to provide for immediate needs, but also to create opportunities for the needy to become self-sustaining economic contributors. This is trickier than writing a check, as it requires real sacrifice of our time and resources. For example, it requires great faith to spend time in mentorship relationships that cross class divides, or to invest in entrepreneurial ideas that may or may not succeed.

And yet, if we trust God to provide for our needs, it frees us to use our influence and resources to provide opportunities for others. Furthermore, if someone's trust in God does not lead that person to act for the benefit of others in need, James suggests that such a person doesn't really trust God at all. As James puts it, "Religion that is pure and undefiled before God, the Father, is this: to care for orphans and widows in their distress" (James 1:27). Belief means trust, and trust leads to long-term invested action.

 *Food for Thought*

What kinds of opportunities allow individuals and families to break free of the cycle of poverty? What well-meaning outreach activities restrain equality and long-term economic benefits?

_____

_____

_____

_____

_____

_____

_____

James's call to give needy people what they need can take many forms, from writing checks that fund good work to going across the world to train medical doctors in poor communities. In what ways can you create opportunities that alleviate long-term need?

_____

_____

_____

_____

_____

_____

_____

Prayer

Jesus,

I lift up the many people of this world who are in great need. Please give me eyes to see specific ways that I can be your hands to help hurting people. I want to follow you in action as well as in love—to make a difference wherever I go.

Amen.

Lesson #3: The Economics of Love

God's word is for all of his people across all time and spheres of living. This includes modern economics. Since relationships of economic exchange tie us together with one another, all Scripture pertaining to relationships is applicable to economic activity. For instance, consider Paul's words on love:

> If I speak in the tongues of mortals and of angels, but do not have love, I am a noisy gong or a clanging cymbal. And if I have prophetic powers, and understand all mysteries and all knowledge, and if I have all faith, so as to remove mountains, but do not have love, I am nothing. If I give away all my possessions, and if I hand over my body so that I may boast, but do not have love, I gain nothing. Love is patient; love is kind; love is not envious or boastful or arrogant or rude. It does not insist on its own way; it is not irritable or resentful; it does not rejoice in wrongdoing, but rejoices in the truth. It bears all things, believes all things, hopes all things, endures all things. Love never ends. (1 Cor. 13:1–8)

Although we may not often think about love and economics in the same breath, love is precisely the addition our theological tradition needs to bring to the world of economics. Work, productivity, financial investment, and value creation are not spheres of activity separate from Christian theology. Rather, the Christian perspective of love, which ties all people together in relationships of trust and integrity, is sorely needed if we want all citizens in our societies to experience abundant life.

The question of how we relate our Christian faith to economic life is important. The work that we do is part and parcel of this world of economy. We can celebrate the different ways we are already participating in influencing economic life, helping to bring fullness of life in a fallen and hurting world. The economic arena does not simply revolve around resource management, but is a sphere of human life in which we can pursue creating a real sense of building a home for humanity.

When we come out of our churches onto the streets and into the markets, seeking the flourishing of all people, God will be glorified. We will make a difference in our own work, in our society, and in economies near and far. The world is watching.

 Food for Thought

While our theology does not solve specific economic problems, it does offer us a godly basis for biblical thought and action. How would you approach this question: Are certain economic systems more biblical than others?

_____

_____

_____

_____

_____

_____

_____

In what ways can love inform your actions at work and in your communities? How does your faith relate to economic life in ways that can potentially advance a more abundant life for all?

_____

_____

_____

_____

_____

_____

_____

Prayer

Father,

Thank you for giving me a part to play in bringing your fullness of life to the lives of others. I ask that your Holy Spirit motivate all my actions with the love of Jesus.

Amen.

Wisdom for Using This Study in the Workplace

Community within the workplace is a good thing and a Christian community within the workplace is even better. Sensitivity is needed, however, when we get together in the workplace (even a Christian workplace) to enjoy fellowship time together, learn what the Bible has to say about our work, and encourage one another in Jesus' name. When you meet at your place of employment, here are some guidelines to keep in mind:

- *Be sensitive to your surroundings.* Know your company policy about having such a group on company property. Make sure not to give the impression that this is a secret or exclusive group.

- *Be sensitive to time constraints.* Don't go over your allotted time. Don't be late to work! Make sure you are a good witness to the others (especially non-Christians) in your workplace by being fully committed to your work during working hours and doing all your work with excellence.

- *Be sensitive to the shy or silent members of your group.* Encourage everyone in the group and give them a chance to talk.

- *Be sensitive to the others by being prepared.* Read the Bible study material and Scripture passages and think about your answers to the questions ahead of time.

These Bible studies are based on the Theology of Work biblical commentary. Besides reading the commentary, please visit the Theology of Work website (www.theologyofwork.org) for videos, interviews, and other material on the Bible and your work.

Leader's Guide

Living Word. It is always exciting to start a new group and study. The possibilities of growth and relationship are limitless when we engage with one another and with God's word. Always remember that God's word is "alive and active, sharper than any double-edged sword" (Heb. 4:12) and when you study his word, it should change you.

A Way Has Been Made. Please know you and each person joining your study have been prayed for by people you will probably never meet who share your faith. And remember that "the LORD himself goes before you and will be with you; he will never leave you nor forsake you. Do not be afraid; do not be discouraged" (Deut. 31:8). As a leader, you need to know that truth. Remind yourself of it throughout this study.

Pray. It is always a good idea to pray for your study and those involved weeks before you even begin. It is recommended to pray for yourself as leader, your group members, and the time you are about to spend together. It's no small thing you are about to start and the more you prepare in the Spirit, the better. Apart from Jesus, we can do nothing (John 14:5). Remain in him and "you will bear much fruit" (John 15:5). It's also a good idea to have trusted friends pray and intercede for you and your group as you work through the study.

Spiritual Battle. Like it or not, the Bible teaches that we are in the middle of a spiritual battle. The enemy would like nothing more than for this study to be ineffective. It would be part of his scheme to have group members not show up or engage in any discussion. His victory would be that your group just passes time together going through the motions of a yet another Bible study. You, as a leader, are a threat to the enemy, as it is your desire to lead people down the path of righteousness (as taught in Proverbs). Read Ephesians 6:10–20 and put your armor on.

Scripture. Prepare before your study by reading the selected Scripture verses ahead of time.

Chapters. Each chapter contains approximately three lessons. As you work through the lessons, keep in mind the particular chapter theme in connection with the lessons. These lessons are designed so that you can go through them in thirty minutes each.

Lessons. Each lesson has teaching points with their own discussion questions. This format should keep the participants engaged with the text and one another.

Food for Thought. The questions at the end of the teaching points are there to create discussion and deepen the connection between each person and the content being addressed. You know the people in your group and should feel free to come up with your own questions or adapt the ones provided to best meet the needs of your group. Again, this would require some preparation beforehand.

Opening and Closing Prayers. Sometimes prayer prompts are given before and usually after each lesson. These are just suggestions. You know your group and the needs present, so please feel free to pray accordingly.

Bible Commentary. The Theology of Work series contains a variety of books to help you apply the Scriptures and Christian faith to your work. This Bible study is based on the *Theology of Work Bible Commentary,* examining what the Bible say about work. This commentary is intended to assist those with theological training or interest to conduct in-depth research into passages or books of Scripture.

Video Clips. The Theology of Work website (www.theologyofwork .org) provides good video footage of people from the marketplace highlighting the teaching from all the books of the Bible. It would be great to incorporate some of these videos into your teaching time.

Enjoy your study! Remember that God's word does not return void—ever. It produces fruit and succeeds in whatever way God has intended it to succeed.

> "So shall my word be that goes out from my mouth;
>   it shall not return to me empty,
>   but it shall accomplish that which I purpose,
>   and succeed in the thing for which I sent it." (Isa. 55:11)

"This commentary was written exactly for those of us who aim to integrate our faith and work on a daily basis and is an excellent reminder that God hasn't called the world to go to the church, but has called the Church to go to the world."

BONNIE WURZBACHER

FORMER SENIOR VICE PRESIDENT, THE COCA-COLA COMPANY

Explore what the Bible has to say about work, book by book.

THE BIBLE AND YOUR WORK
Study Series